Table of Contents

INTRODUCTION

A nyone seeing me walk down the street would never imagine the world I inhabit. Drumbeats, turntables and fiery flows fuel my environment. My world is the rap world. But in my realm I am an outsider, an invisible man of sorts who observes and interacts with people as much a part of the culture and the business as I am. Yet I know that I will never be able to cross over the gulf that sets me apart.

Sure, I own more than 15,000 rap albums and have been listening to the music devoutly since I was about 10 years old. I have attended hundreds of rap concerts, gone to even more hip-hop clubs, written more than 2,300 articles on hip-hop culture and have worked as an editor at Rap Pages (where I was Features Editor) and The Source (where I was both Senior Editor and Executive Editor). Beyond the rap media, I've written about rap in The New York Times, Los Angeles Times and Rolling Stone. My first book, 2006's *The History of Rap and Hip-Hop*, is an overview of the evolution of hip-hop culture and rap music. I've been thanked on more than 25 rap albums and mentioned (positively, might I add) in at least two rap songs.

Sadly, though, there is little chance for me to be fully accepted in my industry of choice, even by those who know far less than I do about the subject. There's a very simple reason for all this.

I am white.

The *I'm The White Guy* series of books aims to provide an insider's view from an outsider's perspective into the rap world, the world I love. Yes, I may not look the part, but I am hip-hop to the core.

There must be an ulterior motive to my love of hip-hop, many people (both white and black) have suggested over the last 28 years of my life. They're wrong.

I developed an interest in rap music when I was about 10. As a rock music fan, my father had exposed me to the merits of the Beatles and many of his other favorite artists. (He had taught me the value of music one day when he arrived home from work and found me using his albums as Frisbees.) But in 1985 when a friend introduced me to artists such as Doug E. Fresh and the Get Fresh Crew, LL Cool J, Run-DMC, Whodini and U.T.F.O., my appreciation for such contemporary rock acts as Europe, Poison and the Bangles evaporated. With this new sound, my life started changing dramatically.

To date, I have interviewed Dr. Dre, Eminem, Jay-Z, Ice Cube, Lil Wayne, T.I., Ludacris, Snoop Dogg, OutKast and Kanye West, among many others. I've written and produced for VH1, worked for Fuse and have been featured on camera on VH1, ESPN, E! Entertainment and Fuse, all where I'm commenting on the intricacies and inner workings of the rap world.

So, as you read *I'm The White Guy* know that you're getting a first-hand look into an exclusionary world from a person who has had to convince people (and hasn't always been successful) of the legitimacy of his love for the genre, as well as his legitimacy to be viewed as legitimate.

The *I'm The White Guy* series kicked off with *The Tech N9ne Edition*. I brought out the big guns for the second installment, *The Jay-Z*

I'M THE WHITE GUY

THE JOURNEY OF SOREN BAKER'S LIFE AS A WHITE RAP JOURNALIST

THE SNOOP DOGG EDITION

BY SOREN BAKER

Takoma Ridge Media

I'm The White Guy – The Snoop Dogg Edition

Copyright © 2013 by Orange Line, Inc.

Published in the United States of America.

Cover Design By Lewn. www.facebook.com/lewnmusic.

Photos © Orange Line, Inc.

E-Book ISBN 978-0-9846912-6-5

Print ISBN 978-0-9846912-7-2

First Edition: April 2013

Edition. Now it's time to take it to California for *The Snoop Dogg Edition.*

I first met Snoop Dogg in Virginia in 1997 when he was on the rock-heavy Lollapalooza tour. I was there to interview him for the now-defunct Beat·Down magazine. Since then, I've been to three of the Long Beach rapper's houses, hung out with him in multiple cities and gotten to know him well. This edition focuses on my conversations and interactions with Snoop, my observations on my time spent with Snoop and my insight and reflections on the evolution of his career.

And with that, welcome to my world. The rap world, where *I'm The White Guy* – always was and always will be.

CHAPTER 1

WHO AM I
(WHAT'S MY NAME)?

I have been listening to rap virtually non-stop since about 1985. I enjoyed the music in all its various incarnations, but in late 1988 and early 1989 my world was rocked by the release of Eazy-E's *Eazy-Duz-It* and N.W.A's *Straight Outta Compton* albums. Although the gangster rap of Schoolly D and the hard-edged, politically-minded material of Boogie Down Productions, Public Enemy, Big Daddy Kane and others was among my favorites, Eazy-E and N.W.A took the best elements of rap and blended them into a revolutionary mix. They were raw yet articulate, angry yet measured, raunchy yet informed, humorous yet serious and, perhaps most importantly, unapologetic about every one of those qualities.

Eazy-E was N.W.A's business mind (and owned Ruthless Records, which released N.W.A's and his albums), but he also added authenticity (he famously used the money he earned from dealing drugs to launch his label) and humor to the group. Ice Cube was the crew's conceptual genius, bringing political, societal and street-level insight in ways that had never been delivered in rap. MC Ren was the rugged, angst-filled foil to both Eazy-E's prankish persona and Ice Cube's deep-thinking, reflective scorn. Yella served as the group's quiet ambassador, manning the turntables and drums on recordings, as well as co-producing the albums.

Then there was Dr. Dre.

Dre's aural muscle propelled N.W.A's often raucous lyrics, as he was the sonic mastermind of the group. He worked with long-time collaborator Yella (the pair were one-half of The World Class Wreckin Cru before joining N.W.A) to assemble some of rap's most angry, driving, funky music to that point. Of course, Dre rapped, too, delivering one of N.W.A's best songs on his solo showcase "Express Yourself," an ode to believing in yourself and your work.

But N.W.A's reign was nearly as short as it was influential. After Ice Cube departed the group in 1989 in order to launch a solo career, N.W.A enjoyed commercial and mainstream acclaim in 1990 with the *100 Miles And Runnin'* EP and the *Eazfil4ggin* album a year later, but the group lost much of its lyrical depth, creativity and significance with Ice Cube's departure.

On the musical side, Dr. Dre's production was improving and he worked with a growing list of talented artists on the Ruthless roster (The D.O.C. and Above The Law, among them), but with no Ice Cube. He needed what he had lost – a gangster-rap partner-in-rhyme.

That void was soon filled.

When Dr. Dre launched his solo career in 1992, he wasn't exactly riding solo. On the menacing "Deep Cover" single, the good doctor introduced the then-Snoop Doggy Dogg as his new protégé. "Deep Cover" was the theme song for the Bill Duke-directed 1992 film of the same name starring Laurence Fishburne and Jeff Goldblum. The movie follows Fishburne's character's journey as an undercover police officer trying to bring down Goldblum's character, who is a drug trafficker.

Over a sinister bassline, punishing piano chords and brutal drums, Dr. Dre and Snoop Doggy Dogg delivered a harsh tale of killing undercover cops. Dr. Dre had gone from saying "Fuck Tha Police" with N.W.A to killing undercover officers with his new sidekick.

But where Ice Cube and MC Ren were unapologetically brash, confident and confrontational, Snoop Doggy Dogg favored a laid-back approach on the mic. The Long Beach rapper's rhymes were delivered with a chilled, almost detached confidence that worked well with the song's tale of killing an undercover police officer.

With "Deep Cover," his first post-N.W.A release, Dr. Dre proved that, like Ice Cube, he could thrive after leaving the self-proclaimed "world's most dangerous group."

Dre also showed that his ear for talent remained razor sharp, as Snoop Doggy Dogg's remarkable performance on "Deep Cover" instantly made him one of rap's most intriguing up-and-coming artists.

In December 1992, Dr. Dre released his debut solo album, *The Chronic*, on Death Row Records, Dre's label with Marion "Suge" Knight. Like "Deep Cover," the LP was hardly a solo affair. On it, Dr. Dre was joined by Tha Dogg Pound, a conglomerate of artists anchored by Snoop Doggy Dogg. In reality, *The Chronic* was as much a showcase for Snoop as an artist as it was for Dr. Dre the rapper. Snoop appeared on virtually every song, as well as the collection's biggest singles, "Nuthin' But A 'G' Thang," "____ Wit Dre Day (And Everybody's Celebratin')" and "Let Me Ride."

I was infatuated by the vocal interplay between Dre and Snoop, as well as Tha Dogg Pound's RBX, Dat Nigga Daz, Kurupt and The Lady Of Rage. Where Ice Cube infused his gangsterism with a healthy dose of political commentary, Dre's new crew only offered social commentary on such selections as "The Day The Niggaz Took Over" and "Lil' Ghetto Boy."

It was Christmas season 1992 and I was asked to bring *The Chronic* to a house party in Crofton, Maryland. It was my senior year in high school and, by that point, all my classmates knew that I had all of the best, latest rap music. Although many of the parties I went to at the time were attended by a wide cross section of students (read plenty of white *and* black students), I remember being surprised that the kids throwing the party wanted me to bring the album since they were the type of white people who typically didn't listen to much rap and certainly didn't embrace its more abrasive incarnations.

So it wasn't much of a surprise that as soon as I popped in the cassette and Snoop Dogg started barking at listeners over some grating, high-pitched keyboard, dropping the *f* and *n* bombs quickly and repeatedly on "The Chronic (Intro)," that several of the girls at the party looked painfully uncomfortable and several of the guys who didn't care for rap were whispering among themselves.

It was as if the white girls were saying, "Man, why does Soren always bring his rap music to our parties?" For the guys, I imagined they were saying, "Man, why are we listening to this when we've got U2, Red Hot Chili Peppers and Nirvana?"

But for whatever reason, no one asked me to change the music, so I simply let the album play. Then something special happened: as the album played and "Let Me Ride" and "Nuthin' But A 'G' Thang" soon arrived, *The Chronic* served as the soundtrack to the evening. This was gangster rap of the most potentially objectionable nature, to be sure, but it was delivered so slickly and so non-confrontationally thanks in large part to Snoop's laid-back delivery and the LP's heavy reliance on funk samples, that the more people at the party listened to it, the less it seemed to bother them. It wasn't that they were tolerating it, though. They were embracing it.

As *The Chronic* emerged as one of 1992's most heralded albums of any genre, Snoop Doggy Dogg prepared for the release of his debut album. In November 1993, I was wrapping up the first semester of my freshman year at Xavier University in Cincinnati and Snoop's *Doggystyle* made history for two decidedly different reasons. It became the first debut album to enter the pop music charts as the No. 1 album in the country. It was also the first time that an artist who was on trial for murder had the No. 1 album in the country.

Snoop was eventually found not guilty in his murder case, while *Doggystyle* went on to sell more than 5 million copies, more than *The Chronic.* "Gin And Juice," "Murder Was The Case," "Who Am I (What's My Name)?" and "Doggy Dogg World" ruled video shows and radio programs well into 1995, making Snoop Doggy Dogg rap's preeminent star.

Snoop's charisma was undeniable. He appeared to be a thin, shy guy who oozed charm and who existed almost accidently in the chest-thumping world of hard-core rap. He showed his player side in the "Doggy Dogg World" video and on the fan favorite "Ain't No Fun," establishing himself as a sharp-tongued rapper who balanced menace with womanizing and comedy.

I would soon meet him.

CHAPTER 2

FREESTYLE CONVERSATION

I was making steady journalistic strides while enrolled as a full-time student at Xavier University. In 1995, I started writing for The Source (the preeminent hip-hop culture publication at the time), Rap Sheet (a national rap newspaper) and several Cincinnati publications, including Everybody's News (an alternative weekly newspaper) and the Cincinnati Herald (one of the city's black newspapers). I was starting to interview and write feature stories about a number of prominent rap acts, including The Fugees, Kool G. Rap and Poor Righteous Teachers, adding an extra layer of excitement to my career. Rather than just writing about the albums and commenting on their quality, I was now interviewing artists and writing extensively about them for prominent publications.

As I was establishing my base in the journalistic realm, Snoop's popularity was hitting stratospheric heights. *Doggystyle* became a bona fide cultural phenomenon. He appeared on two songs from 2Pac's landmark *All Eyez On Me* double album. Released February 13, 1996, the chart-topping collection was buoyed by Snoop's sizzling appearances on fan favorites "2 Of Amerikaz Most Wanted" and "All About U."

More significantly, Snoop was acquitted of murder charges on February 20, 1996. Freed from the lingering legal issues, he was now ready to enhance his status as one of rap's top dogs.

But as the victories continued piling up, Snoop faced his first career obstacle when Dr. Dre departed Death Row Records shortly after Snoop was found not guilty. His former producer launched his new venture, Aftermath Entertainment, as Snoop worked on his second album. 2Pac was then killed in a still-unsolved murder in Las Vegas in September of 1996.

So, three years after *Doggystyle* was released and the departures of Dr. Dre and 2Pac, Snoop was now the lone superstar on Death Row Records. It was a turn of events that was as dramatic as it was remarkable. It also set Snoop up for the high-pressure position of being asked to release an album without Dr. Dre and after 2Pac's death. Moreover, he had become the flagship artist of a label once regarded as rap's premier imprint.

Snoop's second album, *Tha Doggfather* was released November 12, 1996. On *Tha Doggfather* song "Freestyle Conversation," Snoop dealt head-on with what the rap world wanted to know: could he be as significant an artist without Dr. Dre's beats behind him. "So that's what makes me now?" Snoop asks rhetorically before profanely saying he didn't care about a beat.

Ultimately, *Tha Doggfather* was neither as potent nor consistent as *Doggystyle*, but it still had superior moments, in particular "Vapors," his reworking of the Biz Markie classic. As he had done by covering Doug E. Fresh and The Get Fresh Crew featuring M.C. Ricky D's "La-Di-Da-Di" on *Doggystyle*, Snoop had taken something taboo in rap – covering a song – and made it cool. That's what visionary artists do: change the landscape.

Like Snoop, I also was trying to make my own mark. But I was having much more modest results, of course. By the summer of 1997, my career was taking off. I'd been interviewing a steady stream of rap's elite – Wu-Tang Clan, OutKast, KRS-One, Erick Sermon, The Geto Boys and 8Ball & MJG, among others – as a regular contributor to The Source, Rap Sheet and One Nut, among others. I was also getting to interview a number of my favorite rappers in person, a major step for me.

Since 1987, I'd dreamt about talking with rappers. Now I was getting to meet them and talk to them at length about their music, their lives and their careers – and getting paid for it. Rap Sheet had flown me to New York to interview De La Soul and Hits Magazine coordinated a Los Angeles jaunt for me to interview Westside Connection, of which Ice Cube was a member.

I was always trying to expand my reach, so I regularly queried any music magazines I wasn't writing for. I'd mail them my articles and offer my services. Beat·Down Magazine, a burgeoning New York-based rap publication, offered me a dream assignment as my entrée to the publication: an interview with Snoop Doggy Dogg.

People in the music industry always seemed happy – and surprised – when they met me. I was told that most people thought that I was black given my phone conversations with them. I have a deep voice and, when discussing rap, I use the appropriate terminology, slang and phraseology as part of my normal conversation. My passion for and near-encyclopedic knowledge of rap didn't hurt.

Snoop would get to look at me, so he'd know I was white and I'd done in-person interviews before, but getting to meet Snoop brought its own set of distinctive circumstances. I was ecstatic about the opportunity, but rap was going through a tumultuous period in mid-1997. 2Pac and The

Notorious B.I.G. had both been murdered within a six months of each other. So, even though he had a platinum album to promote, Snoop had canceled his 1997 tour.

Nonetheless, Snoop found a way to get out on the road. He was going to be in Bristow, Virginia, as a part of Lollapalooza, the rock-centric tour that was trying to reach fans of other demographics. Rap's violent aura created a sinister specter and Snoop traveled to and from each of the 34 dates in a bulletproof van. After the deaths of both 2Pac and Biggie and his allegiance to 2Pac and status as a Death Row artist, Snoop's decision seemed to be a sound one.

I made the 75-mile trip from my parents' house to Bristow July 2, 1997, to interview Snoop. I'd been meeting and talking to artists I'd idolized for nearly three years at this point, but none of them had the combination of massive record sales, controversy and cultural impact that Snoop Doggy Dogg had had at that point in their careers. Moreover, none of them were traveling in a bulletproof van while on tour.

When I got to the venue, Snoop was playing basketball with his crew on a makeshift court in a parking lot. For a man seemingly and justifiably worried about his safety, he seemed carefree and happy while playing ball with his friends and members of the tour staff.

This was one of my first glimpses into the actual life of an artist on the road. I didn't get to see Snoop engaged in any anxious or pensive moments and from the outside looking in, it seemed great to be able to travel around the country, get paid to perform and play basketball during your downtime. The rap life seemed like a grand one.

Later, when it was time for me to meet and interview Snoop, I was beyond excited. Since I'm white and was young, I always made a point to say something or ask a question that let the artist know right off the bat that I know what I'm talking about. I didn't want them to think I was some uniformed dude. I was there because I loved the music.

With Snoop, our conversation began with and naturally included an in-depth discussion of Los Angeles rap. As our discussion continued, we covered the careers of artists that predated Snoop, iconic West Coast figures such as Ice T and King T, among others. But because I knew as much about and had as much enthusiasm for King T, a tremendously talented and pioneering Compton rapper who never became a household name, as I did the far more popular and familiar Ice T, I could see that Snoop was becoming more and more engaged in our conversation and increasingly impressed with me.

Then Snoop unintentionally paid me a tremendous compliment. "You from LA, man?" Snoop asked me. I had only been to Los Angeles once, and that was a two-night trip to interview Westside Connection in 1996. But because of my knowledge of the city's rap culture, Snoop thought that I had to be from there. I just knew too much about it to be from somewhere else. After all this was 1997. It was long before social media and prior to the emergence of the Internet as a resource where even the most obscure factoid can be found.

When I told Snoop I was from Maryland, I could tell that he almost didn't believe me. Here I was a 22-year-old white guy from Maryland who was having an in-depth conversation with Snoop Doggy Dogg about the rich legacy of Los Angeles rap. We had met less than an hour earlier, but Snoop knew that I had a deep appreciation for LA rap and that I could hold my own in a conversation with him about it – someone who lived there as it was being created and was one of one of its biggest practitioners.

17

Soren Baker and Snoop Dogg at the Bristow, Virginia stop of the Lollapalooza tour on July 2, 1997.

With my time with Snoop up, I was leaving with something far more valuable than a great interview. I was departing with the confidence that comes when one of your heroes salutes you and your knowledge.

The next time I met Snoop, he let me know how big of an impression I'd made on him.

CHAPTER 3

STILL A G THANG

The next time I met with Snoop Dogg, both of our lives had changed dramatically, in very different ways.

In March 1998, I landed a dream job: features editor of Rap Pages Magazine. I relocated to Los Angeles from Maryland for the post and, for the first time in my life, I felt as though I was living at my full potential. I was in a rap hotbed, an epicenter for the music and for entertainment in general. I was on salary at a rap magazine and was getting paid to help run a rap magazine, to assist in coming up with its vision and voice and to help execute that vision by assigning, coordinating, editing and writing several articles every month. I was going out four or five nights a week to concerts, music industry events, movie screenings and dinner with movers and shakers in the music and film industries.

And, after feeling like a failure when I graduated from Xavier without a job and moved back to Maryland to live with my parents, I was living on my own, finally fully self-sufficient. It was a blissfully reality, one filled with rap virtually all day, every day. It was like a dream come true.

My father reminded me soon after I was in Los Angeles that I actually was living my dream, or at least accomplishing one of my main goals. He pointed out that in my high school yearbook I'd put that one of my goals was to deal with rap music every day. Now I was – and I had a full-time job in Los Angeles doing it.

I also felt a tremendous sense of validation. In college, I had to deal with questions about my affinity for rap from both white and black people who didn't know me and didn't understand the depths of my passion for the music. I felt as though my rap knowledge, my ability to write compelling copy and my skills editing the work of others made me an ideal candidate for the Rap Pages gig. Thankfully for me, Allen S. Gordon, who hired me (and who happened to be black), felt the same way. My being white didn't matter to him.

When I got to Los Angeles I put all my focus on mastering my position as features editor. Once I got used to the flow of working at a monthly magazine, I got back to freelancing. I had been doing it since 1995 and made sure that my boss at Rap Pages wouldn't mind if I freelanced as long as I didn't write for our competition and I got all of my work done on time.

Given that Rap Pages was my first full-time job and that I was a 22-year-old white guy helping to run a major rap publication, I was met with some skepticism, however. Two of my co-workers, both of whom happened to be black females, challenged my rap knowledge in front of other staff members, prompting me to improvise a rhyme inspired by Snoop Dogg's "Gin And Juice" to some of my more supportive co-workers: "With so much drama in the LFP, kinda hard being the white boy Soren B." (LFP was short for Larry Flynt Publications, which published Rap Pages.) The questions I faced were, at this point in my life, little more than an annoyance. After all, I had other things more significant to focus on.

Thus, in May 1998, I sent the Los Angeles Times copies of my work from the New York Times, Chicago Tribune and other outlets, and had some of my friends who were publicists put in a good word for me with editors at the Times. Later that month, I started writing for the Los Angeles Times. In June, I began writing features for the paper, whose daily circulation was 1 million and 1.3 million on Sunday.

I was living the best of both worlds. Through my day job at Rap Pages, I got to work with a staff of people who loved hip-hop culture and rap music specifically. As a freelancer, I got to pitch and write stories and review albums that maybe I couldn't for whatever reason at Rap Pages.

In July 1998, I got to write a feature on Snoop Dogg, as he was now known, for the Los Angeles Times. I went to interview him July 21, just over a year since I'd last met him. His life had been totally upended in the previous 12 months.

Gone was the bulletproof van he used on the 1997 Lollapalooza tour. Also absent was a somewhat restrained and slightly edgy Snoop. Of course I had only met him the one time, but when I sat down with him July 21, 1998 on the downtown Los Angeles set of his *The Game of Life* movie, he seemed much more at ease than he had in Virginia the year prior.

Snoop was smiling, laughing and seemingly having the time of his life with some of his friends when I arrived for my interview in Los Angeles. Once I saw Snoop, I said, "I met you in Virginia last year. We were talking about King T." "Yeah, I remember," Snoop said to me with a smile as he extended his hand to me. "You know your shit."

As I switched into interview mode, I had to focus on some dramatic changes in Snoop's life and career: he had lost his good friend 2Pac and switched labels, going from Death Row to Master P's then-red hot No

Limit imprint. All the upheaval was dramatic and nerve-racking, but Snoop seemed truly at peace as he talked in his signature soft-spoken manner.

"I went through a lot of tragedies, a lot of growing up . . . a lot of development," he told me that day. "I lost a lot of friendship, a lot of companionship. I went through a lot since the last album. This album, I went into it with a clear head, free mind . . . ready to do just good music. Nothing really concerns me right now [other than] staying true to what I do and thanking God for every moment I breathe and walk this Earth. You've got to enjoy life, man. Going through things like [I have], it betters the person. You've got to go through some downs to come up. It helped strengthen me up mentally, physically and musically."

Snoop indeed seemed rejuvenated. In addition to the impending release of his third album and his new film, he had appeared on well-received albums from Master P, Mystikal, Silkk the Shocker and C-Murder, heightening the buzz for Snoop's own material. Whereas some questioned his viability without Dr. Dre, Snoop was again primed to be a rap force.

As we talked in his trailer, it was clear that Snoop Dogg was happy with his life and comfortable talking to me about the ups-and-downs he'd been through in his six-year career in the public eye.

"I developed into a full-grown man in front of the public and musically I developed," Snoop said to me a few moments before stepping out of his trailer and shooting a scene in his movie. "I am happy. I'm able to work in an environment where everybody is just strictly [about] music."

As was the case with some of my better interactions with artists, I felt an adrenaline rush as I was leaving. I'd just concluded a tremendous interview with one of rap's biggest stars for one of the nation's biggest newspapers. Even though I was on foreign land, I felt at home, welcomed and embraced for who I was and what I brought to the table as a rap fan and as a writer.

My Los Angeles Times article on Snoop Dogg, "Lost Dogg Found," ran in the Los Angeles Times August 1, 1998, four days before his *Da Game Is to Be Sold, Not to Be Told* album arrived in stores. My editor at the Times, Robert Hilburn, held the article in such high regard that he put a copy of it on the wall in his office.

The next time I met with Snoop, I'd be seeing the pictures on his walls.

CHAPTER 4

BETTA DAYS

The longer I was in Los Angeles, the more I loved it. There was a magical sense of accomplishing something I'd been dreaming about since 1987 – talking and hanging out with rappers – and I was doing it on a near-daily basis. Add in making more than a livable wage for a single man and free access to virtually any entertainment event I wanted to attend and it's easy to understand why the City Of Angels was my favorite locale. I was able to live the life I'd always dreamt about. My job was an extension of that.

The magazine business works months in advance, so in early April 1999, Rap Pages was working on its July 1999 issue, which would come out in June 1999. Virtually all magazines adhered to this faux calendar, in order to make the magazine seem ahead of the time, I guess, but it was just confusing and seemed unnecessary to me. If a magazine was coming out in June 1999, for instance, I didn't see a reason to be ahead of the curve and label it the July 1999 issue.

Regardless, it was early April 1999 and Rap Pages needed a cover subject for its July 1999 issue. The cover story, after all, is the most important part of the magazine. It is often the reason a casual consumer would buy the mag at a newsstand and it's also the reason subscribers would wait with anticipation for the next issue of their favorite magazine to arrive in the mail – to get a prime story on a person or topic of particular interest to them.

Several of our cover stories had fallen through for one reason or another, so I pitched the following to my boss, executive editor Allen S. Gordon: we do a split cover, one with Snoop Dogg and the other with Eightball & MJG. The reason to have two covers was that Snoop would boost Rap Pages' sales nationwide and Eightball & MJG would carry us in the South. I suggested that we would each write one of the cover stories. I was a huge fan of both artists and had already interviewed both, so if Allen liked the idea, it would be a win-win for me and for the magazine. We'd get Snoop Dogg, one of rap's premier acts, on the cover, as well as Eightball & MJG, one of the South's most significant acts, some well-deserved shine, too.

What was most remarkable – and I realized it as soon as the words detailing my off-the-top-of-my-head idea came out of my mouth – was that I was actually in a position to have the idea, pitch it to someone who could make it happen and then be a part of actually making it happen.

Allen thought it was a great idea and on April 10, 1999, I was driving to Claremont, California, to interview Snoop Dogg at his house there. Claremont is a small, quiet city about 35 miles east of Los Angeles. I'd never heard of Claremont, let alone been anywhere near that area, so I was intrigued to see it, especially since Snoop Dogg lived there.

When I got to Snoop's neighborhood, it was quiet, quaint and looked like an upper-class suburban area. As I walked up to the house and its wrap-around driveway, I was surprised and impressed by the dog imagery that adorned the fences around the property. These were the first signs that the property was owned by someone willing to amend its luxurious exterior. The house seemed larger and nicer than most than I'd ever been in, but I was more focused on talking to Snoop than surveying his property. Snoop did a great job of promoting the place, though, featuring its 6,527 square feet, eight bedrooms and full basketball court on a 2000 episode of MTV's *Cribs*.

I didn't get to see nearly that much of the house, but when one of Snoop's boys told me to meet him in the studio in the back of the house, I walked through a hallway and that featured Snoop in family portraits with his wife and two children. I was stunned.

Even though I knew that rappers, like anyone else, had families and loved ones, I was still getting used to seeing artists as people, not just entertainers I'd hear on a song, see in a video or playing a role in a movie. I quickly reminded myself that this was Snoop Dogg's *house*, where he lived with his wife and children. He looked peaceful and full of pride in the family photos, something different than how he often portrayed himself to the public, where he was brash, confident and occasionally menacing – all the while soft-spoken and ultra-cool.

When I got close to the studio, the door to the room opened and smoke began wafting from the room and into the living room area where I was. A few seconds later, Snoop Dogg emerged. It seemed mythic almost, this lanky, legendary rapper emerging from the marijuana smoke from his home studio into the rest of his serene, sanitized house.

"What up, nephew?" Snoop said to me with a big smile on his face. I was at total ease. I no longer had to prove myself to Snoop. He knew me and was comfortable with me. I was there to have a quality conversation with Snoop about his career, his forthcoming *No Limit Top Dogg* album and anything else that came up.

I was particularly curious about why Snoop – who had sold more than 9 million albums with his first three releases and who was one of the biggest rap artists of all time – would collaborate with No Limit's lesser artists, like Gambino Family and Prime Suspects. His answer provided a blueprint to how Snoop would operate for the next decade-plus.

"It opens up to let the fans know that Snoop Dogg's going back to where he started from," he said to me. "He doesn't think he's too big so that he'll only do songs with the big artists that sell millions of records. He's about breaking new artists, too. That's what it's about on No Limit, helpin' each other. I'm cool with that. I was helped in the game, so I don't have any problem helping somebody else in the game."

Few rappers I'd ever met had that type of humility, even the ones who'd yet to release an album. Snoop Dogg, did, though, which I think has been a key to his success. He's willing to work with anyone he thinks is talented, who is working toward achieving their own goals.

As the conversation continued, it naturally gravitated toward Snoop's work in the community and his work in youth football, among other things. I then asked him how fatherhood had changed him. His answer stunned me and provided me with tremendous insight into my life and those who I often wrote about.

"I wanna live," he said. "Point blank. I wanna live. That's a good place to start."

I'd never thought about my desire to live. Living was something I expected and took for granted. My parents provided a safe, comfortable upbringing for me in Gambrills, Maryland, while Snoop was raised in the gang-infested east side of Long Beach. He'd been a gang member, dealt drugs, been tried for attempted murder, had several friends killed and been a central figure in some of rap's biggest feuds.

Other than a few isolated incidents, I never had to deal with that type of chaos in my life. Snoop's answer gave me pause. I felt blessed and appreciative for my life, something I essentially took for granted. Now, that Snoop had achieved a certain level of peace, he realized what it was like to have something to live for.

Snoop Dogg seemed to be in a good place personally and professionally, possibly more so than at any point in his life. When he played me select songs from *No Limit Top Dogg*, Snoop also seemed back in his creative comfort zone. His unmatched combination of gangsterism, wit and cool returned in ways not demonstrated since 1993's *Doggystyle*. The Dr. Dre-produced "Bitch Please" with Xzibit was a bona fide hit, as was the C-Murder- and Magic-guested "Down 4 My N's," which C-Murder even appropriated and eventually used as his own single. "Just Dippin'" with Dr. Dre and Jewell and the Dana Dane remake "Snoopafella" were other standout cuts that showed that Snoop remained one of rap's marquee acts.

My "Barking Up The Right Tree" piece on Snoop Dogg was the cover story of the July 1999 issue of Rap Pages. Even though my whiteness had long been an issue with some people, I was beginning to feel as though people were simply treating me for who I was: a die-hard rap fan and emerging writer who happened to be white.

As one of my black female friends from high school would later tell me, "I never thought of you as black or white. You were just Soren." My next interaction with Snoop Dogg went a long way to making me think people in the entertainment industry were starting to feel the same way.

CHAPTER 5

FROM THA CHUUUCH TO DA PALACE

I like to save money whenever possible, so I typically brought my lunch to work at Rap Pages. I rarely went out to lunch and it became a bit of a joke around our office that I always brought my fruit and homemade turkey sandwich for my midday meal.

One day in fall 1999, I decided to go out to lunch with a publicist. When I returned to the office, there was a strange vibe. People looked sad, as if someone had died.

No *person* had died, but on the one day I went to lunch, the executives at Rap Pages came down to let us know that they were shutting the magazine down. My world changed dramatically during my 60-minute absence.

Like the rest of the staff, I was stunned. The publication was growing in ad revenue by double digits every year and our circulation was also growing at a robust rate. We were also getting more and more marquee artists on the cover of the magazine despite the stranglehold industry standard The Source had on the marketplace.

From what I was told by a variety of people within the company, the Flynt executives wanted more commercial acts on the cover on a more regular basis and didn't understand why we weren't growing at the same rate as The Source.

Regardless, less than two years into my dream job, it was over. I was 3,000 miles away from my family and out of full-time, salaried work.

Fortunately, I had had a robust "second job" as a freelancer with the Los Angeles Times and others and had already developed a strong support system and network of friends in Los Angeles. Chief among them was Billy Johnson Jr. He had been the first one to hire me on a regular basis as a writer when I was in college when he was an editor at Rap Sheet. He was now at Launch Radio Networks.

Billy helped me land a job at Launch as Editor, Urban West Coast. In that post, I conducted interviews and wrote news items that appeared on a variety of radio stations around the country. I also resumed writing for The Source, XXL and the other rap magazines that had been Rap Pages' direct competition.

But I never fit in with the Launch culture and decided to take a chance on love, so at the end of 2000, I moved to Chicago. I was putting my career and everything I'd worked hard for since college in jeopardy, but love will do that to you. Besides, I had it worked out that my then-fiancé and I would move to either Los Angeles or New York so I could have the best chance for my career to thrive once she completed medical school. I always envisioned Chicago as a pit stop rather than a permanent location.

Fortunately, Launch had a Chicago office, so I stayed on with them for a few months until they were able to replace me with someone in Los Angeles. I had been writing for the Chicago Tribune since 1997, so I started writing for them on a more regular basis now that I was local. With my newfound location in the Midwest, I was a go-to guy for The

Source, XXL and Vibe, among others, when they needed to cover someone in the region, which also included the South.

My career was solid, though it took a major step forward in March 2002 when VH1 called and asked me if I'd like to write and produce an *Ultimate Albums* episode on Eminem's *The Marshall Mathers LP*. Of course I did.

I was going to conduct the interviews for the episode, write the script and, in essence, be the creative lead for the show. But I had to relocate to Los Angeles to do it. So my friend Richie Abbott let me sleep on his floor for two months while I worked on the project. Like I said, I had a great group of friends in Los Angeles.

Among the people I told VH1 producers Daniel Soiseth and Greg Heller I could get for the episode was Snoop Dogg. They seemed overjoyed that I could land a Snoop interview for the program, so when I got to LA in April 2002, I started setting it up. This time, I would be interviewing Snoop at one of his houses in Diamond Bar, California. It's about 30 miles east of downtown Los Angeles, making it about a 40-mile trek from VH1's Santa Monica offices. No one seemed to mind the distance, though. We were going to Snoop Dogg's house, after all.

We were set to interview Snoop at 4 pm. The crew was excited and anxious to meet the iconic artist. As this point, Snoop had also started flexing his acting chops, appearing with Denzel Washington and Ethan Hawke in the Oscar award-winning *Training Day* and with Tyrese Gibson and Taraji P. Henson in John Singleton's *Baby Boy*. In other words, Snoop Dogg was no longer just a rapper. He was a superstar.

But as 4 pm turned into 5 pm and then 6, I was getting nervous. I had no doubt Snoop would show – we were at his house, after all – but I started getting calls from the VH1 office. "Where is he," they wanted to know. "Was he going to show up? Every hour beyond 6 pm we have to start paying overtime and then triple time."

I tried not to show it, but I was scared out of my mind. Here I was working on a dream project only to end up costing the show tons of extra cash waiting around for one of the key interviews for the program. I tried to convince myself everything would work out.

At about 8 pm, it did when Snoop Dogg finally showed up.

Everyone's angst evaporated almost instantly and Snoop Dogg gave us one of the episode's best lines. When I asked him what he thought about Eminem's song "Kim," in which the Detroit rapper describes killing his wife, Snoop said, "Shit, who doesn't feel like killing their motherfuckin' wife every now and then?"

No one other than the subject is supposed to make any noise when doing an on-camera interview, but nearly everyone in the room erupted in laughter. Snoop had taken the discussion of a grisly song and spun it into something hilarious. That's what makes him so remarkable: his ability to make virtually anything into something funny, as well as memorable.

Remember, this is an interview about Eminem's *The Marshall Mathers LP*. Snoop appeared on the collection's "B**** Please II," a remake of his 1999 hit, and had toured with Eminem, but after about 30 minutes of the interview, Snoop said, "C'mon, Soren. You're asking me all these questions and are only going to use me for about two minutes in the whole show."

Again, Snoop had me cracking up. He was right, too. So, I wrapped it up with another question or two.

Snoop Dogg and Soren Baker at Snoop's house in Diamond Bar, California for Snoop's interview for VH1 Ultimate Albums episode on Eminem's *The Marshall Mathers LP* in 2002.

Snoop then took another 30 minutes to talk with and take photos with the entire VH1 crew. It ended up being a spectacular night filled with laughs and, most importantly, an incredible interview with Snoop Dogg.

As I was heading back to Richie Abbott's place, my thoughts turned from elation to panic. I realized that I had run into triple time with the crew. I was worried I'd get fired from the show.

I showed up to the office the next morning bracing for the worst. To my pleasant surprise, no one said anything about the overtime expense or making everyone wait around for hours.

"That's great you got Snoop," Daniel Soiseth said. "I hear the interview went great, too."

I then realized getting Snoop was what ultimately mattered. No one ever mentioned the overtime to me and with Eminem, Snoop Dogg, Dr. Dre, Xzibit, Jimmy Iovine, Billy Johnson Jr. and others in the show, the VH1 execs appeared thrilled with the final product.

The *Ultimate Albums* episode I wrote and produced on Eminem's *The Marshall Mathers LP* debuted on VH1 June 16, 2002. I watched it back in Illinois.

When the closing credits appeared, I got a little misty-eyed. I was taking the next step of my career, writing and producing for television. Amazingly, Snoop Dogg, one of the biggest entertainers on the planet, helped make the experience a remarkable one for me and a hit program for VH1. The episode aired regularly for about five years after its debut.

My next noteworthy encounter with Snoop was at a gathering of extraordinary gentlemen.

CHAPTER 6

SUITED N BOOTED

I'd been living in Chicago since the end of the year 2000 and the Windy City, for those that don't know, stands as a long-time fixture in the world of black street pimps. One of the scene's most famous flesh peddlers is The Arch Bishop Don Magic Juan. The Chi-Town native is – or isn't – a reformed pimp now serving as a preacher and spiritual mentor who gained national notoriety via two 1999 documentaries on pimps, *Pimps Up, Ho's Down* (which featured him on the cover of the DVD with two women kneeling at his side) and *American Pimp.*

Given that rappers grew up on the same streets that produced pimps, it's natural that the two groups have long admired each other. Oakland, California's Too $hort was the first rapper to regularly discuss the world of pimps and prostitutes in his music, a practice he started in the mid-1980s. But the other pimp-centric songs of the era were more about pimping as a concept than as a practice.

In 1987, Los Angeles rapper Ice T imagined himself as someone living the glamorous side of a pimp-like lifestyle (excessive jewelry, several women at his disposal and an endless supply of flashy clothes) on "Somebody Gotta Do It (Pimpin' Ain't Easy!!!)." Big Daddy Kane's 1989 tune "Pimpin' Ain't Easy" was more about having sex with women than actually pimping. Ice Cube, on the other hand, presented a brutal, realistic portrayal of the pimp-prostitute relationship in the first verse of his 1990 song "Who's The Mack?" before discussing other situations where everyday people get pimped. (Pimps are sometimes referred to as macks).

Soon thereafter, however, the pimp persona itself started becoming commonplace in rap. The Pomona, California rap group Above The Law named its 1991 EP *Vocally Pimpin.*' The Port Arthur, Texas rap duo UGK, consisting of rappers Pimp C and Bun B, broke nationally in 1992. Memphis rap duo 8Ball & MJG featured the songs "Pimps" and "Pimps In The House" on their debut album, 1993's *Comin' Out Hard.* A year later, Oakland rapper Dru Down had a rap hit with the single "Pimp Of The Year" and in 1996 Chicago rap trio Do Or Die launched their career with the single "Po Pimp."

For his part, Snoop Dogg had been peppering his lyrics since 1993's *Doggystyle* with the language, slang and phrasing commonly used by pimps, players, hustlers and other street characters.

As for me, my exposure to the real world of pimps and prostitutes was limited to what I'd seen in movies, on television and heard in rap music. I'd observed what I was sure were pimps and prostitutes outside, in and around strip clubs during my rare trips to them, but I'd never utilized any of their services.

While I was virtually oblivious to the world of pimps, The Arch Bishop Don Magic Juan, or The Bishop for short, had been a celebrity magnet since at least the 1980s. By the 1990s, he had become friends with gangster rap pioneer Ice T, and, later, Snoop Dogg. Snoop featured The Bishop in *The Wash,* also starring Dr. Dre, the 2001 feature film that Snoop executive produced. The Bishop also appeared in 2002's

Snoopadelic Films Presents: Welcome To Tha House – The Doggumentary DVD.

By 2001, pimping was in vogue in rap, in large part due to the alliance of Snoop and The Bishop. That was especially evident on the October 20, 2001 tour stop of the Puff, Puff, Pass... tour, which Snoop headlined. My review of the show, "Snoop Dogg Life Of The Party" ran in the Chicago Tribune October 22, 2001.

In my review, I described Snoop's pimp-like attire at the show, which included a calf-length mink and matching hat. He also wielded a gaudy gold goblet. When you factor in Snoop's pressed gray suit and dark sunglasses, anyone who did not already know who Snoop was might have mistaken him for a pimp – especially since The Bishop and several other pimps joined Snoop on stage during his lively 80-minute set that night.

I'd met with Snoop and The Bishop at Snoop's house during a June 2002 trip to Los Angeles, so I was familiar with their relationship as well as the Bishop's place in rap, and was interested in doing a story on them. In November 2002, Snoop released his sixth studio album, *Paid Tha Cost To Be Da Bo$$*. Snoop decided to celebrate the release of his new LP by attending The Bishop's birthday party in Chicago.

I asked the Chicago Tribune if I could cover the event, which also doubled as a Player's Ball, an annual congregation for pimps, hustlers, entertainers and athletes that has been taking place on The Bishop's birthday since the 1970s. I'd been hearing about the Player's Balls for years and thought it would make for an interesting story.

To my surprise, the Tribune said yes. So on November 30, 2002, I met Snoop Dogg and The Bishop at the Sutton Place Hotel in downtown Chicago before heading to the party at East of the Ryan on 79th Street on the city's South Side.

Snoop Dogg, Soren Baker and The Arch Bishop Don Magic Juan at one of Snoop Dogg's Diamond Bar, California houses in 2002.

By the time I got to his hotel, Snoop was dressed in full pimp attire: an eye-catching, ankle-length burgundy leather coat with white mink highlights, a customized burgundy sweater, a platinum chain with the logo of his Doggy Style Records and small-framed glasses.

Although Snoop was a husband, father and an A-List music celebrity making significant inroads into television and film, he had no qualms about embracing pimping, especially its more romanticized aspects. After all, he'd grown up hearing about the Player's Balls and enjoyed such pimp-centric films as 1973's *The Mack*. Snoop told me what drew him to the pimp culture. "It was the beautiful women, the outfits. The way they dress, the cars, the money. It was just the whole persona and knowing you look good and when you look good, it feels good to look good. It makes you feel a little better."

With several beautiful women hanging at his arm, a camera crew following him and several of his friends from California by his side, it was easy to see why Snoop was so enamored with the lifestyle and why he'd wanted to attend The Player's Ball.

I followed Snoop's caravan to the event, which was a star-studded affair. Rap stars such as Lil Jon, Da Brat, Big Daddy Kane, Daz Dillinger and RBX mingled with funk legend Bootsy Collins and blaxploitation star Dolemite. It was more of a celebration of The Bishop and his pimp friends. Pimp awards are handed out at each one of the Player's Balls, making it part party, part tribute, part recruiting function and all-around spectacle.

It's also a celebration, one in which the women have little role. The girls, as seems to be the case in the pimp-prostitute relationship, are clearly an afterthought at The Player's Balls, little more than an accessory

Snoop Dogg and Soren Baker at the 213 album cover photo shoot in Los Angeles, California on October 9, 2003.

for the various men whose arms they hang on. That reality makes attending a Player's Ball less objectionable. It's an extremely sanitized glimpse into a segment of society that reflects one of the worst types of male-female relationships, though you'd never know it in the midst of the celebration.

My article documenting Snoop's trip to The Player's Ball, "The Pimp Lifestyle Is Right Up This Dogg's Alley," ran in the Chicago Tribune December 4, 2002.

I moved back to Los Angeles in 2003 and I'd met up with Snoop Dogg soon thereafter for the 213 (his group with Nate Dogg and Warren G) album campaign, among other times during the next several years, but it was a 2007 interaction that gave me a new perspective into Snoop's significance.

BOSS' LIFE

In 2006, I authored my first book, *The Music Library: The History Of Rap And Hip-Hop*, which came out in April. After listening to rap full-time since about 1985, this was a major milestone for me. Ice Cube and Xzibit were among the rappers who raved to me about the book and also seemed happy for my getting to the next stage of my career.

I was also the Senior Editor of The Source and, as had been the case during my stints with Rap Pages and Launch Radio Networks, I continued freelancing and working on my outside projects, which at this point also included writing and producing DVDs for Tech N9ne and Chingy, among other things.

Since meeting up with Snoop a few times during the 213 album campaign, he had arguably become more popular than ever. In 2004, he released the smash *R&B Rhythm & Gangsta (The Masterpiece)* album, which included the blockbuster single "Drop It Like It's Hot" as well as popular cuts "Let's Get Blown" and "Signs" with Charlie Wilson and Justin Timberlake. He also appeared in the hit films *Starsky & Hutch* and *Soul Plane* that year, among other acting gigs.

Snoop released his *Tha Blue Carpet Treatment* album in 2006. In addition to being one of my favorite albums of the year, I thought that it was remarkable that 13 years into his solo recording career that Snoop Dogg was still releasing top-tier material. In the fast-paced rap world, being among the genre's elite for *three* years is amazing. Maintaining that A-List status for 13 years is stunning.

On April 10, 2007, I went to meet with Snoop at a Los Angeles recording studio near Hollywood to discuss his forthcoming *The Big Squeeze* compilation. The set featured rappers Kurupt, Westurn Union (the trio of Soopafly, Damani, Bad Lucc), War Zone (a group consisting of rap veterans MC Eiht and Kam and Eastsidaz member Goldie Loc) and JT Tha Bigga Figga, as well as R&B singer Azure.

The LP was remarkable for several reasons, most prominently that Snoop produced the majority of the album under his producing moniker Niggaracci. The beats were spare and funk-heavy and definitely solid if you're into that sound and style.

As noteworthy as Snoop's move into production was, *The Big Squeeze* also gave me a chance to reflect on all the work Snoop had done to help other artists. He'd put out a gold and a platinum album with his side group Tha Eastsidaz and compilations featuring a host of his own artists through his Doggy Style imprint when it was with MCA Records, as well as the 213 album in 2004.

Snoop had also sold more than 17 albums as a solo artist at that point, but other than a handful of artists who had been out since the 1990s (Dr. Dre, Ice Cube, Xzibit) and the more recently emergent The Game, there were few Los Angeles area rappers – especially gangster rappers – who were making significant waves musically and professionally. Of them, Snoop was the only one making an active push to promote a stable of artists.

Despite Los Angeles gangster rap being one of rap's best-selling and most influential subgenres since the late 1980s, in 2007, few companies wanted to release material from artists making that type of music. Snoop realized this and decided to put himself on the line as a promoter and recruiter of LA-based artists.

"Until I did this record, none of these guys had nothing ready to come out," Snoop said to me in the studio that day. "Nobody was knocking on their doors saying, 'Hey, man, when's your album coming out? I want to give you this opportunity.' So, this is me just bum-rushing the game, squeezing the game right now, saying, 'Forget that. Ya'll going to listen to this right now.'"

Longtime Snoop Dogg affiliate Soopafly was particularly appreciative of Snoop's effort with *The Big Squeeze*. "He's the only one looking back and really reaching out to those that don't have it," Soopafly said of Snoop that day. "He understands West Coast music the best, more so than any label."

Possibly more so than any other artist, too. Snoop had been a regular fixture on other artists' albums – both major and independent – since he left Death Row Records and signed with Master P's No Limit imprint in 1998. Beyond his appearance on dozens of albums during that stretch, I'd often reflected on his 2001 Puff, Puff, Pass... tour. Snoop brought unheralded veteran rap trio Tha Liks on that jaunt, even though their music is more traditional rap than gangster-styled like Snoop's and even though their notoriety and record sales aren't in Snoop's stratosphere.

I don't know the behind-the-scenes business of how the tour line-up came about, but the bottom line is that Snoop brought Tha Liks, an immensely talented LA-based rap group who releases high quality music, on the road with him. Snoop had long been reaching out and lending a helping hand to artists far less prominent than he was, providing these acts with opportunities to keep living their own dreams. That may not have been the case without Snoop's assist.

The Big Squeeze came out through KOCH Records, an independent label with major label reach. Even though the album hadn't come out when I interviewed him, Snoop had the same plan whether it became a hit or it was a dud.

"All these labels call me when they get ready to put an artist out and they need a hot single or Snoop on a verse, but they won't give me that look for my people, so I had to really just be effective and efficient and say, 'You know what, I'm not going to wait on nothing because it's the same game every time,'" Snoop said to me. "I just decided to produce this record, put it out and shoot dice like I always do. If it crap out, we'll shoot again. If it hit, we'll still shoot again. That's what we do."

Snoop seemed genuinely happy to help artists who came out before he did (MC Eiht, Kam), artists he'd long been working with (Soopafly, Goldie Loc) and help up-and-comers (Damani, Bad Lucc, Azure) get exposure in ways that they wouldn't have enjoyed otherwise. Few artists with a 13-year run in the rap game had the opportunity to do that, and of them, only Snoop Dogg was doing it on such a regular basis with such a large and ever-evolving number of artists.

My article on Snoop Dogg and *The Big Squeeze*, "Snoop Dogg wears even more bling," ran in the Los Angeles Times April 25, 2007, marking a decade in my relationship with Snoop Dogg.

CHAPTER 8

MY OWN WAY

I spent a lot of 2007, 2008 and 2009 on the road, so I didn't see Snoop much during that time. We'd cross paths at events and would share a few laughs when we'd see each other, but he seemed busier than ever, expanding further into the television and film worlds while continuing to release high quality music on a regular basis.

Snoop gave fans an intimate look into his family dynamic in late 2007 when *Snoop Dogg's Father Hood* debuted on E! Entertainment Television. It was the side of Snoop I'd seen in 1999 when I went to his Claremont, California home to interview him for Rap Pages and had seen the family portraits adorning the walls of his hallways.

I'd also got to meet his children and got to see him interact with them in early 2003 at one of his Diamond Bar, California homes when I went to interview him there for King Magazine. The story was about his line of Snoop DeVille cars with Cadillac that he was doing at the time.

Every other time I'd hung out with Snoop, he'd been around his friends and other rappers more so than his family, so it was revealing to see Snoop interact with his children, especially his daughter Cori. Even though Snoop had been widely criticized for the portrayal of women in his music throughout his career as well as his affinity for pimping, Snoop was everything you'd want a father to be when he was speaking with his daughter: kind, patient, attentive and compassionate.

It's a side of Snoop that he's displayed throughout his career, even if it has received little notice from fans and critics. One of my favorite lesser-known Snoop songs is "I Believe In You," a soulful, Hi-Tek-produced cut from his 2002 album, *Paid Tha Cost To Be Da Bo$$*. The tune features R&B singer LaToiya Williams, another Snoop protégé, playing the role of Snoop Dogg's woman, singing to him about how much they believe in each other. In his lyrics, Snoop discusses how much he loves the woman that would become his wife. It's a rare rap love song that features a stellar beat, strong lyrics and an uplifting message without a drop of corniness. It's grown-folks rap.

As fans, we often forget that the people who create the art we appreciate so much are actually people, too. They may play a role in a movie, act up on reality television or portray a particular persona in some of their music, but they also have families, feelings and emotions. They're not characters. They're real people.

I've always made a point to realize this. I became involved in the music industry because I am a fan of the music. I hope my work reflects that.

I will discuss non-music related topics with artists when they're relevant, of course, but as my first encounter with Snoop in 1997 taught me, my love for and knowledge of rap goes a long way with the people I interview and work with.

That standing in the game helps me to sustain my career, or at least plays a role in it. It also enables me to have access to some tremendous events that have given me some of the best memories of my professional career. In 1999, for instance, I was flown to Hawaii to cover the Dr. Dre and Snoop Dogg reunion concert sponsored by Los Angeles radio station Power 106.

A little more than a decade later I went to another exclusive event. In 2010, Snoop announced that he'd be releasing his *Doggumentary* album the following year. I got invited to his private listening event at Capitol Records in Hollywood February 18, 2011 to listen to selected songs from *Doggumentary* and to hear him discuss the LP.

As Snoop previewed such selections as "Wet," "My Own Way" and "My House" with Young Jeezy and E-40, virtually everyone in attendance seemed impressed with the music. My former The Source colleague Ryan Ford hosted a Q&A where Snoop discussed the new album and why the LP evolved away from Snoop's original idea of a sequel to *Doggystyle*, his landmark 1993 debut album.

"The reason why I chose *Doggumentary* for the title of my record is because it was more of a documentary that I was actually doing at the time of making my record," Snoop said at the event. "It was like I was documenting my career, my music, my videos, the whole nine. So instead of calling it *Documentary*, I said, 'You know what, let me put the two Gs on 'em and call it the *Doggumentary* to make it more the way I do me.' So, I just took that and enhanced as opposed to trying to recreate *Doggystyle Part 2*, trying to do something that could not be done."

My "Snoop Dogg Documents Upcoming Doggumentary Album" article appeared on RedBullUSA.com February 22, 2011.

CHAPTER 9

THA NEXT EPISODE

In November 2009, my friend Abby O'Neill invited me to a party she was throwing in Hollywood. While we were talking, I noticed that esteemed actor-director Bill Duke was at the event. I asked Abby if she knew Duke, who in 1992 directed the film *Deep Cover*, whose soundtrack introduced the then-Snoop Doggy Dogg to the world. Abby told me that she'd worked with him for a while and that she would be happy to introduce me to him.

Abby introduced me to Duke, giving me a glowing introduction. He seemed impressed and agreed to have a meeting with me. Less than two weeks later on November 27, 2009, Duke and I met for a sushi lunch in Studio City, California.

Like many people my age, I was familiar with Duke through his work as an actor in 1985's *Commando* and 1987's *Predator* with Arnold Schwarzenegger. Then, a year after directing *Deep Cover*, Duke delivered what is probably his most famous rap-related role when he portrayed a slick yet forceful detective in the acclaimed urban gangster classic *Menace II Society*.

Given this history, as well as his memorable, scene-stealing roles in *Payback* with Mel Gibson and in Steven Soderbergh's award-winning *The Limey*, both released in 1999, I was elated to be meeting with Duke, given my own film and television aspirations as a writer, producer and director. I left the meeting even more impressed with him than I imagined I would be. He'd been acting on television since before I was born and had been a Hollywood mainstay as an actor since the 1970s and as a director since the 1980s, but he is among the most level-headed, considerate and gracious people I'd met – especially in the entertainment business.

Duke felt strongly enough about me and my work to agree to work with me. By the top of 2010, we started collaborating on projects. He featured me in his acclaimed 2011 documentary *Dark Girls*, which explores the biases and attitudes about dark-skinned women in the United States and around the world.

Duke and I have several film and projects in various stages of development and on January 3, 2013, I got what could be a career-altering voicemail message from him. "I had lunch with Snoop Dogg today," Duke said on my voicemail. "He has a script idea. He said he knew you. He said you're friends. He likes you and thinks you'd be the perfect writer for it. I want you to give Snoop a call and we can talk when you get time. Thanks."

I could hardly believe the message when I listened to it. I listened to it again and again before calling Duke back. Duke seemed as excited about the possibility as I did. The plan, as he explained it, would be that Duke would direct the film that Snoop would star in and that I would write.

This is the kind of scenario I've dreamt of my whole life: working with some of my favorite artists on a *creative* level. Now I wasn't going to be writing about their work. I was going to be part of making the work itself.

Duke gave me Snoop's newest e-mail address and I e-mailed him with my current info. I went to Maryland with my daughter about a week later. While I was in Target with my father picking up some supplies for my daughter, Snoop called me from India. He told me that he was going to reach out to me once he got back into the country so he could tell me about his idea for the script and so that he, Duke and I could meet about getting the project off the ground.

Snoop, who had rechristened himself Snoop Lion and who embraced Rastafarianism in 2012, was in full promotion mode at the time as he prepared for the release of his *Reincarnated* documentary and album, his twelfth studio album. We exchanged e-mails for a while and then, on March 21, 2013, Snoop called me. We had a tremendous 20-minute conversation about his film idea.

After we spoke about the concept, I told Snoop I'd call Bill in order to set up the meeting. Snoop then paid me an ultimate compliment. "I really want you to write it, man" Snoop said to me. "I don't want to go no further than this. I think you can write this motherfucker and I think he [Bill Duke] can direct this motherfucker and we can roll and have a motherfucking Academy Award-winning movie."

I told Snoop how much I appreciated his thinking of me for this. Given that I had Snoop on the line and I wanted to ask him if it would be cool if I did an *I'm The White Guy* book on our relationship.

"You've got my blessing," Snoop told me. "Everything we've done, I've loved. That's why when Bill brought you up, I was like, 'I know Soren, man. That's a good guy. We can definitely do this shit.' I didn't shoot you down and say, 'Nah, I don't want to fuck with him. Let me go find a black writer.' I was like, 'I fuck with him, so if you fuck with him, Bill, I fuck with him.' So, if that's what you want to do with the book, I'm all in. Make it happen."

So, that's how Snoop gave me the blessing for this edition of *I'm The White Guy.*

Since March, I've been in contact with Snoop a few times because he wants me to talk to a couple of his relatives for research regarding our film project. We're also setting up a good time for Snoop, Bill and me to meet about the script.

As is usually the case, I'll be The White Guy in the meeting.

Fa sizzle.

ABOUT THE AUTHOR

Soren Baker (far right above, interviewing Snoop Dogg July 22, 2000 at the Hartford, Connecticut stop of the Up In Smoke Tour) has had more than 2,300 articles published in such publications as the Los Angeles Times, Chicago Tribune, The Source and RedBullUSA.com. The Maryland native has penned liner notes for albums by 2Pac, Ice Cube and others, and has worked on television programs for VH1 and Fuse. He has sold a movie script and is the author of 11 other books, including 2011's *I'm The White Guy – The Tech N9ne Edition* and *I'm The White Guy – The Jay-Z Edition*. Baker also co-authored with Game *The Making Of Game's The R.E.D. Album*. He is also working on a film project with Snoop Dogg and Bill Duke. Follow Soren Baker on Twitter and Instagram @SorenBaker.